A ROADMAP FOR IMMIGRATION TO US

Useful Information For Anyone Seeking US Citizenship

Patrick Long, Esq.

Jacobs & Whitehall
73-03 Bell Blvd, #10
Oakland Gardens, NY 11364
(888) 570-7338
www.jacobsandwhitehall.com

Ordering Information:

Quantity sales. Special discounts are available on quantity purchases by corporations, associations, and others. For details, contact the publisher at the address above.

Orders by U.S. trade bookstores and wholesalers. Please contact Jacobs & Whitehall: Tel: (888) 991-2766 or visit www.jacobsandwhitehall.com.

Printed in the United States of America

Published in 2021

ISBN: 978-1-954506-24-4

PREFACE

A lot of lawyers talk about wanting to help the disadvantaged with their work. I doubt any area of law offers as much opportunity to do that as immigration. As an American, it's often easy to get caught up in one's own life challenges, and not really appreciate how good one has it. Whatever disadvantages one may face in life, being born in a peaceful and prosperous country is a powerful privilege. As I write this, the average American, adjusted for spending power, is about 4x as rich as the world average, and about 10x the average for the countries most of my clients come from. This difference in material wealth does not even account for the risks of violence in many countries--from gangs, from domestic abusers, from terrorists, or even from the government itself. During law school, I was unsure of what I wanted to do afterward. I continued working in politics for a while and found myself starting a practice and unsure what to do after the 2014 elections. When a friend asked me to work on some immigration cases with her, I readily accepted the opportunity, and I fell in love with immigration. Helping a client move from a poor or violence-prone country into the US, or avoid being sent back to such a country, is a powerful way to improve that person's life, as well as to enrich the American experience for all of us.

Americans often overlook how much we benefit from having immigrants here. Funny story--I grew up in Knoxville, Tennessee--a strong Trump country. A lot of people there were all for deporting immigrants--until a member of the family that owned a popular local Mexican restaurant wound up in removal proceedings. Countless customers of the restaurant had been supporting stricter immigration policy, all while enjoying the benefits of having this immigrant family in town. This incident is emblematic of the way many Americans view immigration, reaping the rewards of allowing immigrants in but wanting to kick immigrants out. I hope that if any native-born Americans pick up this book, it will give them a window into how complex and difficult our immigration system is, and give them some empathy for people who were born into poverty and violence, through no fault of their own, and are just looking for a better life.

The goal of this book is to provide general guidance about what may be possible if you or a loved one are trying to immigrate to the United States or prevent deportation. It is not to provide legal advice. Immigration law is incredibly complex and constantly changing. Some of the information in this book will probably be wrong by the time it is published. Much of it may sound applicable to your situation, but not apply because of some technicality that I have not covered in the book. If you would like to truly understand your options better, you should contact me for a consultation.

DEDICATION

This book is dedicated to all of my immigration clients, past, present, and future, and to the American Dream. Immigration made America a great country, while allowing immigrants to make the most of their own lives. Helping people through that process is one of the greatest joys of my life and I am grateful that you have given me the opportunity.

DISCLAIMER

This publication is intended to be used for educational purposes only. No legal advice is being given, and no attorney-client relationship is intended to be created by reading this material. The author assumes no liability for any errors or omissions or for how this book or its contents are used or interpreted, or for any consequences resulting directly or indirectly from the use of this book. For legal or any other advice, please consult an experienced attorney or the appropriate expert, who is aware of the specific facts of your case and is knowledgeable in the law in your jurisdiction.

Patrick Long Law Firm, PC.

1452 Dorchester Avenue
Floor 4
Dorchester, MA 02122
(617) 718-5550
www.patricklonglaw.com

TESTIMONIALS

"Mr. Long is very honest and he responds to our immigration issues/questions promptly. He is helping me with an immigration case and keeps us informed about our case. I highly recommend Mr. Patrick Law Firm."

– Emad M.

****

"He helped me deal with various Immigration issues. His professional experience and well-developed knowledge of Immigration have solved my problems."

– A Satisfied Client

****

"Listened to our request and was always on top of things making sure everything was running smoothly. I would recommend his services for sure."

– Gerfi M.

****

"I felt comfortable with that decision! My family has been grateful because Patrick has traced to help us getting good possibilities for our case!"

– Oneyda S.

****

Table Of Contents

About The Author

What Is Your Experience Representing Someone Who Is Immigrating Or Facing Removal?

I've been working in immigration law since the beginning of 2015. I started out primarily handling removal defense because that's where the clients were for a new lawyer who didn't have any connections. These people were usually in jail, most after another lawyer had failed them, so they were desperate to try anything, including giving an inexperienced attorney like me a chance. After having success with a lot of these cases, I built up my practice and have since expanded. I continue to do removal defense, but I also do a lot of family-based immigration now.

Why Is Practicing Immigration Law Important To You?

My practice represents an opportunity to help people during a really difficult time. My clients haven't always been given all of the advantages in life. They often come from worse circumstances than someone who was born in America, so their difficulties arise through no fault of their own; they were just born in the wrong place. I am passionate about helping to give people a chance to live in America and have all of the freedoms and opportunities that America offers.

Who Do You Want To Read This Book?

This book is directed toward people who are looking for an immigration lawyer or trying to learn about the issues that they might face when they're going through the immigration process. I don't want to give legal advice in a book because every case is different, every situation is different. Nevertheless, I hope that readers get a flavor of the challenges they're up against and what potential remedies might be. I want people to go into their immigration journey with their eyes open and understand that this is not an easy process. But I also don't want people to become discouraged by the potential challenges. I think having a realistic understanding of both the difficulties and the opportunities from the beginning is important.

CHAPTER 1

WHAT IS FAMILY-BASED IMMIGRATION?

That's any kind of immigration based on your family relationship to someone else. This type of immigrant seeks a green card based on having a spouse, parent, child or sibling who is a U.S. citizen or, in some cases, who has a green card.

Types Of Evidences Families Will Need To Apply For Legal Immigration

It really depends on the nature of the relationship. The first basic purpose of evidence is proving that the person petitioning for the other person has either a green card or U.S. citizenship that would allow them to petition in the first place. The second basic purpose of evidence is to show that the family relationship that's being claimed actually exists. In some cases, that might be really simple. If you're a U.S. citizen petitioning for your sibling and you have the same parents, all you need is your birth certificate, your naturalization certificate (if you have one), and their birth certificate.

Proving the relationship can be more complicated if, for example, you have the same father but not the same mother. You are still eligible to petition for them, but proving that you share a father, especially if he's not on one or both of the birth certificates, can cause problems. Your parents would either have had to be married at the time of birth or your father has to have gone through whatever the country of birth recognizes as the legitimation process for recognizing a child as his. The proof that you'll need in that situation varies from country to country.

The most complicated evidence is usually for marriage-based petitions. The government is very concerned about people entering into fraudulent marriages just for immigration purposes, and so you have to prove that it's a real marriage, which can take a lot of evidence, depending on the whims of the officer reviewing the application and whether they suspect the marriage is false. If you have kids together, that typically makes it a lot easier because their birth certificates will have both of your names. The government assumes that if you have kids together, you must like each other at least a little bit, so they'll accept that as a real marriage.

For couples who don't have children together, that can get really complicated. There's a common-sense standard for evidence, but remember it's common sense in the eyes of someone who doesn't know you and thinks you could be a liar, so you have to prove everything you claim. This can include anything that proves you live together (your lease or a mortgage, utility bills, etc.) and that proves you've merged your finances together (statements from joint bank accounts, cards from your joint insurance carriers, etc.). Photos of you together, affidavits from friends or family who should know about your relationship, and text messages and call logs with each other can also be important—whatever you can think of that proves that it's a real relationship.

Who Specifically Can Be A Sponsor?

The first thing is that the petitioner has to be a sponsor. The question is whether they can sponsor you alone or whether they need a joint sponsor. The government basically doesn't want to admit people who are going to come here and rely on benefits instead of getting a job, so they want someone who can be financially responsible for the immigrant and ensure they are able to live a lifestyle that's reasonably above the poverty level without government benefits. You need to have a household income that's at least 125% of the poverty level for the size of your household (which includes yourself and any spouse or children that live with you). You have a legal responsibility to support the person you're petitioning. If you've already petitioned someone else for a green card and you're still responsible for them, they will count against your household size for the purpose of determining how much income you need to petition for a second person.

If you need a joint sponsor, then the requirements for them are that they have to be a U.S. citizen or a permanent resident who is domiciled in the US, which means they live in the US and plan to remain here. They also have to have enough income that their income (counting the new immigrant as a member of their household) would be above 125% of the poverty level. Those are the requirements, and in theory, anyone who meets those requirements could be a joint sponsor. However, as a practical matter, the government wants some assurance that this person is actually going to live up to their obligations, so an uncle or another obvious family relation or someone with obvious reason to support this person is going to be better than a random friend who lacks an obvious connection.

Chapter 2

Challenges Immigrating Families Might Face

The biggest challenge for a lot of people is just not having a relative who is eligible to sponsor them. A lot of people have this idea that you can just sort of get in line and immigrate, but you actually have to have specific family members in specific relationships to you who are eligible to sponsor you. (More on those relationships later.)

For those who do have the family connections that would make it possible, there are consistently still a few challenges. Anyone who has any type of criminal record or who has previously been in the United States illegally will definitely face challenges based on that. Anyone who has previously applied for any kind of immigration status and been denied might face increased scrutiny. That could be a problem depending on why the prior application was denied, particularly if the government thinks that the person lied to them during that process. Overall, that is a simple overview of the biggest challenges.

Beyond those major challenges, there is also the volatility of law anytime the United States has a change in the president—or at least, a change in the presidential party (Republican or Democrat). When Donald Trump became president, he introduced tons of new regulations and tweaks to the law that changed eligibility standards so rapidly that I could give someone advice on one day, only to discover it was wrong the next day due to the change. There have also been changes transitioning from Trump to Joe Biden, though these changes move generally in a more positive direction. Either way, it's important to keep track of what the law is because you may be eligible for things that you weren't previously eligible for, or you may not have to do paperwork that you would have had to do, and so on.

Finally, situations like the COVID pandemic have resulted in a lot of uncertainty, as well. Issues like border closures add evolving challenges. Even in countries where agencies and embassies are still theoretically open, they may have reduced staffing. I can tell you my general sense of what the staffing situation in USCIS is because it's pretty consistent in the United States, but with the embassies, it will vary depending on which country and what their local situation is. Even when the pandemic is over, the uncertainty could linger. Any kind of emergency situation on a large scale can result in those kinds of problems in the future.

CHAPTER 3

WHO IS CONSIDERED FAMILY FOR IMMIGRATION PURPOSES?

The people you are eligible to sponsor depend on your immigration status. If you are a U.S. citizen, you can petition for your spouse, your child, your parent, or your brother or sister. Children are a little bit of an unusual situation because their category is treated differently based on whether they're over 21 or under 21 and whether they're married or unmarried. US citizens can petition for their siblings, parents, or married children in addition to the other categories;

permanent residents only for their spouse or unmarried children. Again, whether they're over or under 21 makes a difference as to what category they're in, but you can still petition for them as long as they're unmarried. Stepchildren and stepparents are included as long as the marriage that created that relationship happened before the child turned 18.

If You're A Lawful Permanent Resident Who Wants To Bring A Family Member To The US, What Type Of Visa Will They Need?

For someone who's outside the United States, they're going to need to get an immigrant visa as opposed to a non-immigrant visa, which includes categories like tourist visas (meaning there's no intent to remain in the United States). You cannot, however, directly apply for the immigrant visa. In order to apply for an immigrant visa, you first have to file an I-130, which is a petition with some basic information, to establish what the relationship is and that you're eligible to sponsor the person who wants to come here.

And then, once that's approved, you have to go through a whole other process with the National Visa

Center and with the local embassy or consulate of the country that they're coming from. There are different preference categories depending on your immigration status, your relationship to the person you're sponsoring, and their age and marital status. That's an overview of the process. Then, you'll have to submit more documentation to establish the relationship and wait.

Who Can Be A Beneficiary Without Any Numerical Restrictions?

The immediate relatives of a U.S. citizen are not subject to numerical restrictions. People who do not fall under immediate relatives are put into a preference category, and each category has a restriction on how many people per year can be granted a visa under that category. Most of the categories have a backlog, so you might have to wait years until visas actually become available for the year in which you applied. Someone who applied in 2015, if there were no visas available then for their category, will have been waiting for one to become available, and you're waiting behind everyone who applied in that year and 2016 and 2017 and so on.

Again, the exception to this is an immediate relative of a U.S. citizen. For those spouses, parents, or children under the age of 21, the only delay is the actual processing time, which is still pretty significant. In fact, I'd say be prepared for up to two years to get through it all. You can actually speed the process up by having your documents ready, getting them in, and just being prepared at all times. The other categories will face a delay no matter how well their case is put together.

What Other Preference Categories Are There?

They're labelled first preference, second preference, third preference, and fourth preference, but those labels are kind of misleading. Right now, second preference visas, especially F2A visas, are actually easier to get than first preference.

Basically, different types of relatives are split into different categories depending on your status, their relationship to you, their age, and their marital status. First preference includes those unmarried sons and daughters who are over the age of 21 of U.S. citizens. Second preference is actually split into F2A and F2B, and those include spouses and children under the age of 21 (F2A) and unmarried children over the age of 21 (F2B) of permanent residents. Third preference is married children of U.S. citizens; and fourth preference is brothers and sisters of U.S. citizens.

What Does A Sponsor Need To Get This Process Going?

The first things you'll need are the basic documents to prove your status and your relationship to the person that you're sponsoring. You'll need your green card or your naturalization certificate or your birth certificate—whichever proves that you're a permanent resident or a U.S. citizen. Then, you'll need your birth certificate or your marriage certificate to prove that your relationship to the beneficiary is what you say it is. The immigrant applicant will need proof of their status and proof of their relationship.

Beyond that, there is a lot of access to biographical information that's required for the petition. You'll need to provide your parents' names, their dates of birth, where they were born, and the same set of information for the person you're sponsoring. I would say you need to have a conversation with the beneficiary about any criminal or immigration record that they have because you need to be prepared to apply for any waivers they may need. Finally, you'll need the money for the process, for the filing fees and the legal fees.

CHAPTER 4

DOCUMENTS PREPARATION BY U.S. CITIZEN FOR SPOUSE IMMIGRATION

Petitioning for a spouse is always potentially complicated because you have to prove that it's a real relationship and not just a sham for immigration purposes. Proving your U.S. citizenship is probably pretty easy because you'll have your birth or naturalization certificate. Proving that the marriage exists is also pretty easy because you'll show your marriage certificate. Any documents that are in a foreign language need to be translated, and you need to submit both the translation and the original. If either of you has been married before, you need the divorce or death certificate, whichever document shows that the previous marriage was terminated before you entered the current one.

Are The Documents Needed For Other Family-Based Immigration Petitions Similar?

The required documents would be similar. You have to remember that the U.S. government is not going to just take your word for it that you are who you say you are and that you're related to this person how you say you are. Everything that you're claiming needs some piece of paper that says it's true. The more neutral and official the source that paper comes from, the better.

To prove a parent-child relationship, a birth certificate produced by the government is always the best thing. In some countries, however, those don't exist or have only been introduced recently. Maybe you only have the baptism certificate for a child who was baptized a few days after they were born. As proof, that's helpful, but it's not as good as a government-issued certificate. The church is still a sort of neutral authority, one that wouldn't have any incentive to help you lie, and they're in the habit of creating these kinds of records for their own purposes to track who's in their congregation.

In the worst-case scenario, you might have to get affidavits from your friends and family, who would need to say: "Yes, I was there at the birth, and I saw the baby come out," or, "I wasn't at the birth, but the mom introduced me to the baby a day after he was born. I saw that they lived together and she treated him in all the ways that a mother would normally treat her child."

While Their Application Is Pending, Can My Family Member Come To The US?

Generally, they cannot come here. As far as the immigrant visa itself goes, that will not be granted until the process is complete. In theory, there is no rule against them getting a tourist visa or any other sort of status that they might qualify for, but you do have to be careful doing that. The government distinguishes between immigrant intent, which is an intent to come here and live here, versus non-immigrant intent, which is an intent to come here for some limited purpose or limited time before returning to your home country. Applying for any kind of non-immigrant visa while you have a green card process going on can make them kind of suspicious; they might think that you're trying to come here to perhaps jump the line and that you're not actually going to go back to your home country like you're supposed to if you get a tourist visa.

So, they'll be suspicious of it on the front end, and then, if you do come and don't actually leave, that can really cause you a lot of problems. Then, they'll believe that you applied for your non-immigrant visa fraudulently with the intent to not leave and that you lied to them about your intent. In conclusion, while bringing them here can be done, you need to understand that their visa may be denied. If you do get a tourist visa, a student visa, or any other kind of non-immigrant visa, you need to be very careful to obey all the rules and conditions of that visa.

How Will Immigration Determine That My Assets Are Sufficient To Meet The Financial Support Requirements For My Family Member's Petition?

They look at your income from your tax returns, your W2s, and sometimes your current paystubs. Tax returns are good because they provide the opposite incentive of this requirement. When people file their taxes, they want to make their income look as low as possible so they can pay less in taxes, so you don't have the same incentive to inflate your income as you might when you're sponsoring someone. A tax return is a more honest document, and that's why they look at it. If your income is high enough, that often is enough, but if it's close to the minimum, they might want more, such as a current paystub, to prove that you're still making enough income.

If Petition Is Approved, What Happens Next?

The petition, the I-130, is just the first step in the process. Depending on the beneficiary, the next step is either filing an I-485 (which can actually be filed at the same time as the I-130 but won't necessarily be approved at the same time), or the case is transferred to the MBC, and then it goes through the process described earlier. If the case requires any waivers, those have to be decided before the visa can actually be granted, so adjudication of any waiver requests will be an intermediate step between the I-130 and the actual final decision.

CHAPTER 5

WHAT HAPPENS AFTER THE FAMILY-BASED IMMIGRATION PETITION IS SUBMITTED?

You'll get a filing receipt in about a month, but it typically takes six months to a year to get any kind of substantive response. And that's just the first step in the process. That's just the I-130. Requests for evidence are unusual on I-130s, but people do sometimes get them. In most cases, even if there's an issue that could be a problem, they will approve the I-130 as long as your immigration status and the relationship are proven sufficiently. Don't get too excited—you'll still have to deal with the issue later in the process. Even if your I-130 gets approved, you still face obstacles.

Once that's approved, it'll be transferred to the National Visa Center, which takes at least 30 days. (They'll even send you a letter saying, "Do not contact National Visa Center for at least 30 days.") Realistically, it takes more like 60 to 90 days to get transferred, and then, at that point, there's another form you have to fill out, DS-260, which is like the I-130 on steroids. It'll ask you a lot of the same questions, and part of that is just to see if you give the same answers to help screen out people who are lying. If, however, something was wrong originally, you can make corrections, and you *should* make corrections, but you'll need to explain why you did that. Then, there's another documentation that needs to be submitted to the National Visa Center, and that goes to the local embassy or consulate, who will set up the interview.

Do The Sponsor And The Applicant Attend Immigration Interview Together?

Typically, they will not attend together because the government understands that the sponsor is in the United States so they don't need to come to the embassy for the interview. They would most likely be allowed to attend if they wanted to, but that would mean a lot of time and expense for something that's not necessary.

At the interview, they will ask the beneficiary a lot of the same kinds of questions that are on the papers to assess whether they're being truthful or to answer any lingering questions. Particularly when it's marriage-based, they may try to test you on how well you know your spouse. They also want to see the beneficiary and make sure they're actually the person that they claim to be and that they match their passport.

Are We Able To Have Our Immigration Attorney At The Interview?

For enough of an extra fee, you can have your attorney, but that is pretty unusual. It's more common to have your attorney present for your adjustment of status interview, which is when people who are already in the United States are applying for a green card. I charge an extra fee for that.

Whether it's necessary for me to be there depends on the case. I do recommend that I be there for most marriage-based cases, unless it's a really obvious and strong case (such as a couple who has kids together). If there's no question at all about the marriage, having an attorney there may not be necessary. For new marriages, couples who don't have kids together, or couples who've had cheating in their marriage (or anything that might suggest that it's not a real marriage), I think it's better to have an attorney there.

After Interview, How Long Is The Next Waiting Period?

If you're outside the United States, the consulate will make a decision, and if they grant your visa, you can start making your travel arrangements once you have the visa. If they feel that they don't have enough information, they might ask for additional documentation.

If you're inside the US and adjusting your status, they might give you a decision that very day, though not always. Again, they may request more information, so the post-interview process is about the same either way.

Common Reasons That Family-Based Immigration Petitions Are Denied

Probably the most common reason would be the official not believing it's a real marriage in a marriage-based petition. I also see a lot of denials based on criminal records or previous immigration history for people who go through the process without an attorney. Those denials are less common for people who hire an attorney for two reasons.

The first reason is a bit negative. Your attorney can help you decide whether to file the petition *at all*. If it's a weaker case, you might decide not to waste your time and money on a case that doesn't have a chance based on your attorney's advice.

The second reason is that your attorney can guide you through whichever waivers you might need and help you present negative information in a way that is still honest but that doesn't make you look as bad. Attorneys can make legal arguments about, for example, whether a crime is in the category of crimes that would make you ineligible.

In cases involving less-developed countries, there can be issues with the documents that are difficult to resolve. As I mentioned, some countries only started doing birth certificates within the last few decades, and it can be difficult to deal with that and prove whether someone really is your parent or your child without a birth certificate. People who face that alone often don't know how to deal with that issue.

CHAPTER 6

COMMON REASONS FOR A DEPORTATION OR REMOVAL FROM THE UNITED STATES

The most common reason depends on who is president at the time. Democrats like to deport people for having criminal records; Republicans like to deport people for being here illegally. Being in one category or the other doesn't guarantee that you're safe because it's sort of opportunistic. You're still, by law, at risk of deportation either way, but it's a matter of where ICE tends to prioritize using its resources. Typically, when a Democrat is president, ICE will make more of an effort to look in jails and find people who have criminal records to make them removable; and when a Republican is president, they'll make more of effort to find people who are here illegally.

In terms of the way people use the terms nowadays, there may be a difference between deportation and removal. As a legal matter, any proceeding that's initiated today would be a removal proceeding. The law used to call it deportation, but it's the same thing. It's the government trying to kick you out of the country.

How To Know If Someone Is In Danger Of Being Deported Or Investigated?

If you are in the country illegally either because you entered without authorization or because you overstayed your visa, then you're always at some risk of deportation. If you have a criminal record, it really depends on the record, and you need to talk to an attorney about the specifics because certain categories of crime make you deportable even if you have a green card. Broadly speaking, those categories are controlled substance offenses, crimes involving moral turpitude, aggravated felonies, and domestic violence offenses (plus some firearms offenses). A domestic violence offense tends to also be considered either a crime involving moral turpitude or an aggravated felony or both.

Be careful about taking these terms too seriously; this is why I say you really need to talk to a lawyer about it because the term "aggravated felony", for example, covers a lot of crimes that under state law are misdemeanors but are designated as aggravated felonies under federal law. Just because the judge told you that the crime you were convicted of is a misdemeanor, doesn't mean that will be true in immigration. Also, continuance without a finding or anything that involves any kind of admission that you did something wrong could count as a conviction for immigration purposes. If you're worried about the possibility of deportation and you have a criminal record, consult with an attorney. That way, you can at least get a sense whether it's something you need to worry about.

There's not really any way to know if you're under investigation or not. Filing any kind of petition or application with immigration could trigger an investigation. That's why I recommend not filing a weak application—it could result in someone who is removable coming to the attention of the authorities. If you get arrested on any kind of criminal charge, that is also more likely to bring you to the attention of the authorities. There's no foolproof way to avoid coming to their attention. It's often just a matter of luck.

What Are My Rights If ICE Comes To My Home Or Shows Up In A Public Place?

In a public place, you have a right to leave, unless ICE tells you that you don't and that you're under arrest. In your home, you don't have to let them in unless they have a warrant from a judge. They often don't have a warrant from a judge; instead, they'll have a so-called administrative warrant, and that's not the same thing. If you are a target, it may not make a difference whether you let them in or not because, eventually, they will find a way to get you, whether you're on the way to work or at work or whatever. Not letting them in would be more of a protection for other people in your home who you're worried they might find out about. If you are the target and you're the only person who's at risk, then it's often better to just cooperate. They're going to arrest you eventually anyway; just don't give them any information and ask to contact an attorney. You do have a right to an attorney.

You have to divulge any information; you should not lie to them. Anything untrue you say can be used against you later, and anything truthful that you admit to that's bad can be used against you later. Generally, it's best not to answer any of the questions.

Then, you are entitled to a bond hearing in front of a judge, though the burden of proof is unfortunate. In a criminal case, the burden of proof is on the government, so they have to prove that you're a flight risk or a danger to the community to keep you in jail while you're waiting for trial. But with ICE, it's kind of the opposite. You have to prove that you're not a flight risk or a danger to the community. In Boston, there's actually a federal court ruling that says that standard is illegal and that the burden is supposed to be on the government, but in reality, that decision hasn't changed a whole lot about the way the immigration judges have interpreted the law.

CHAPTER 7

THE PROCESS OF BEING DEPORTED OR REMOVED

First, ICE will serve you a notice to appear, or at least, a document that they claim is a notice to appear. There's still an open legal question that the courts are working on about what constitutes a valid notice to appear. Your document will say it's a notice to appear and will tell you that they're placing you in a removal proceeding, as well as what the grounds are for thinking that you're removable. It should have a date and time for your hearing (although they often do not) and where the hearing will be.

What Happens At A Hearing?

There are three basic types of hearings. One is a bond hearing. Something that trips up a lot of people who try to go through this without an attorney is that the bond case is technically separate from their removal case, and so any documents and evidence submitted into the record for the bond hearing are not automatically transferred over to the removal record. Oftentimes, people who don't have an attorney will try to rely on something they submitted for bond, but it's not even in their record to be used in a removal case.

As far as the case on the marriage, there's a master calendar hearing, which is basically a pre-trial or a status hearing for attorneys and the judge to plan out the case and get on the same page. There'll be at least one master calendar hearing, though usually there's more. At the first hearing, if you don't already have an attorney, you can ask the judge for more time to find an attorney. In Boston, they'll usually give you two or three chances to find an attorney and then go forward without one if you haven't found one. I don't have as much experience in other courts, but my understanding is that they do vary. Some of them will just go forward if you don't have an attorney at the very first hearing; they might only give you once chance. Then, once you either do or do not have an attorney and the case is progressing, you have to file pleadings, which is a document that tells the judge whether you agree that the government's accusations that you're removable are true or not. That document also lists what applications for relief you're going to file.

Typically, then there'll be another master calendar hearing to file the applications. They, in theory, are trying to move away from that right now to instead just set a deadline in the calendar, but I don't know how well that project is going to hold up.

Eventually, you'll get to the individual hearing, which will be a trial. All documentation in support of the application has to be submitted well in advance of the individual hearing. Different judges have different preferences on how far in advance (they'll explain that at the master calendar hearing), but all the documentary evidence has to be submitted in advance. Any witnesses have to be ready to go to testify at the individual hearing because you only get one chance to put on your case. If the bond is denied, a case typically takes about 60 to 90 days from the time you're arrested to the time it's decided. If you get bond, then it'll usually be several years.

CHAPTER 8

POSSIBLE DEFENSES TO STOP A FAMILY MEMBER FROM BEING DEPORTED OR REMOVED

If the grounds for removal are not true, you might be able to get the case dismissed based on that. This would be more common when it's a criminal issue because there may be some reason that ICE believes that a crime falls within a category that makes someone deportable, but actually, the crime is not within that category. This is where a good lawyer can really make a difference in terms of making the argument that the elements of the crime place it outside of that category.

If ICE is alleging that you entered without inspection or overstayed a visa, they are usually right about that. If they're alleging fraud, you can contest that, but that's probably an issue that would require an individual hearing because it's pretty complicated. It's not something that's just a matter of a legal argument like the criminal convictions may be. Those are the first aspects to evaluate.

Second would be any sort of insufficiency in the process. I mentioned the issue with a lot of so-called notices to appear not actually being valid notices to appear. Whether that actually helps you or not depends a lot on your situation. Even if you get the case dismissed based on that, they can just bring the case back with a valid NTA. That could, however, provide a form of relief if your cancellation of removal and your eligibility for it depends on how long you've been in the United States before the notice to appear is filed. If you're on the line between eligible and ineligible, getting the case terminated and forcing them to bring it again can actually get you across the line and get you the 10 years that you need to be eligible for cancellation.

Depending on what the case is based on, it may also be possible to get proceedings terminated, which is the immigration term equivalent to dismiss in most state courts. One way to do that will be prosecutorial discretion, which is just ICE agreeing that deporting you is not a big enough priority that they want to continue with the case. That discretion was not available at all during the Trump administration, but the Biden Administration has brought it back. ICE is historically less likely to grant it during Republican administrations than during Democratic ones. Even under Democratic administration, it's only available to some people. Typically, anyone with a serious criminal record is not going to get it; even a minor criminal record might be disqualifying. It does help people who maybe entered the country illegally or overstayed their visa but who have done everything in their life right from that point on. In those cases, it just doesn't make sense to prioritize deporting them.

Some forms of relief are not completely under the immigration judge's control, but they may dismiss the case or administratively close it, which is sort of like a dismissal except that there's still technically a case, though they're not moving forward on it. They might do that to let you apply for a relief you're eligible to apply for with USCIS.

Finally, the last thing would be your applications that do get decided by the immigration judge, so those will depend on your circumstances. If you're a permanent resident, cancellation of removal would definitely be the most common. The eligibility standards are completely different for permanent residents and for people who are not permanent residents—it's unfortunate that they have the same name. LPR cancellation is when the judge has a lot of discretion as long as you meet the basic eligibility requirements. The first requirement is not having a criminal record that would disqualify you (aggravated felonies, basically). Beyond that, you have to have had your green card for at least five years, and you have to have been in the US for seven years. There are some more complicated requirements sometimes around whether certain types of crimes can disqualify you if they're committed before you've met the five-year requirement. Someone who came here before the age of 18 might actually be able to inherit a longer period of residence from their parents.

For non-LPR cancellation, you have to have been in the US for a continuous period of 10 years. You have to have had good moral character during that 10-year period, which basically means not having certain criminal convictions (and there are a lot more types of convictions that can disqualify you, such as crimes involving moral turpitude and controlled substance offenses, for example). The good moral character also means you have to pay your taxes and generally obey the law. More and more judges will deny people who haven't submitted proof of paying their taxes. Also, lying to the government on any previous immigration applications could be a cause to deny your good moral character. You have to, in addition, prove exceptional and extremely unusual hardship to a U.S. citizen or a lawful permanent resident family member, and that's a pretty high standard. That's not the ordinary hardship that would happen anytime a family member's deported; it has to be something special like if you have a child with a special education issue or a medical issue that you take care of and, for whatever reason, the other parent wouldn't be able to handle this alone.

That hardship, along with the kinds of things that would qualify you for asylum, can be good qualifiers that can help you get cancellation of removal. Asylum requires that you either have been persecuted or would be at risk of persecution in your home country, either by the government or by someone who the government is unable or unwilling to control. That persecution has to be based on your race, religion, political opinion, particular social group, or nationality. Asylum can be a lot broader than what it may sound like. For example, a lot of people coming here from Central America may be able to apply for asylum based on persecution by gangs that are so powerful that the government can't control them. Particular social group is sort of vague, so it's possible to make arguments for new particular social groups that the law hasn't previously recognized. And that's always changing. Asylum might also be granted if you're someone who has testified against gang members and would be known to the gang, which would want to persecute you. Those are typically the most common ways to defend against removal.

CHAPTER 9

OPTIONS FOR RELIEF IN AN IMMIGRATION COURT

In addition to the things I already mentioned, there are a few other things that are a bit less common but that still happen reasonably often. If you've committed any kind of fraud, that makes you ineligible to stay in this country, though there are different forms of relief that could potentially be available, depending on what exactly the untruthful statement or document was and where the fraud was in the process. The important thing with any kind of waiver for fraud is that you need to be scrupulously honest. It's better to be honest all the time, but particularly when you've already done something that was false or fraudulent, which makes all your behavior seem suspect. You need to come clean about whatever you've done, ask for the mercy of the court, and explain why you deserve to be allowed to stay in the United States despite doing the wrong thing before.

Committing fraud is a somewhat common thing. In addition to that, people who are already eligible for a green card but who hadn't applied for one can apply to get their green card through the immigration judge. Cancellation of removal for non-lawful permanent residence does get you a green card if it's granted, but there's also adjustment of status based on someone petitioning for you outside of immigration court. You would need a family member who is eligible. They have to file the petition. The I-130 is still decided by U.S. Citizenship and Immigration Services, not the immigration judge, but the I-485, which is the bigger document, is decided by the immigration judge.

What To Do If Cancellation Of Removal Is Denied And All Attempts Have Failed?

There are still a couple of possibilities. The first possibility is what's called voluntary departure, which is kind of a weird term since it's never really voluntary. Nevertheless, it's an alternative to deportation, so you would leave the country, but it wouldn't count on your record the same way that a removal order would count. You can actually apply for pre-hearing or post-hearing voluntary departure. The terms of pre-hearing voluntary departure are a little better, perhaps because they want to encourage people to take it. Typically, however, if someone has any viable opportunity to stay in the United States, I wouldn't encourage them to go for pre-hearing voluntary departure. Post-hearing makes more sense as the last alternative that the judge might give you.

It is still up to the judge, who can choose to order you deported instead, but a lot of times, the judge will grant voluntary departure. The advantage of this option is that you may be able to get back into the United States in the future more easily than if you had a removal order. If you are ordered removed from the United States, that's typically a ten-year bar, but it could even be a permanent bar if you reenter illegally after being deported.

There are a lot of advantages to avoiding a removal order, and it can make sense to accept voluntary departure. It is not, however, a decision that should be made lightly because getting a removal order is the only obstacle that you eliminate by accepting voluntary departure. If you have a criminal record or unlawful presence in the United States (or whatever you're getting deported for), that may also create additional barriers to you being able to return, even if you accept voluntary departure. You would want to consult with an attorney about whether you have a relative who'd be able to petition for you to come back to the US and what your chances of actually getting any waivers that you need would be.

Another possibility is appealing the case. There are actually several stages of appeals that are possible. The first is to the Board of Immigration Appeals, which is another administrative court, like immigration court.

Your appeal would be decided by a judge who is appointed by the attorney general, who, of course, is appointed by the president. The Board of Immigration Appeals is a little more subject to the whims of political processes, but it could still decide your case differently than the immigration judge.

Beyond the Board of Immigration Appeals, you'd appeal to the Court of Appeals for whichever federal circuit you're in. You can appeal certain cases to the Court of Appeals. While all cases can be appealed to the Board of Immigration Appeals (with a few minor exceptions), the right of appeal beyond that is somewhat more limited. You can, for instance, appeal to the Board of Immigration Appeals just based on not liking how the judge decided the case, but there has to be some Constitutional or legal error in the Board of Immigration Appeal's decision to appeal to the Court of Appeals. If such an error exists, you can go to the Court of Appeals and potentially even to the Supreme Court if you lose at the appellate court level. In the Appeals Court, you have a right to appeal to them as long as there's a valid issue, while in the

Supreme Court, you have to ask them to take the case (and they usually won't). So, for most people, the end of the line will either be the Board of Immigration Appeals or the Appeals Court, depending on what the issues are in their case.

That's the standardized, most straightforward path. There are other possibilities, including a motion to reopen or a motion to reconsider. Those motions both go back in front of the same judge who decided the case before. The difference is that a motion to reconsider argues that they made some kind of legal error that you want them to change, while a motion to reopen is based on some kind of factual error (which typically has to be based on new evidence that wasn't available at the time of your hearing for some reason).

There are, at least in theory, pretty strict deadlines on all of those options. The deadline for appeal is 30 days, the deadline for a motion to reconsider is 30 days, and the deadline for a motion to reopen is 90 days. For motions to reopen or to reconsider, there are sometimes more possibilities of filing them after the deadline, if you can make an argument that it's not fair for the deadline to be applied in your case.

If you're below the deadline, you should definitely talk to an attorney right away because you want to get in before the deadline, if possible. If you're beyond the deadline, it would still be a good idea to consult with an attorney and see if there are grounds for an exception to the deadline.

CHAPTER 10

FINDING A QUALIFIED IMMIGRATION ATTORNEY

There's particularly a problem for people from Spanish-speaking cultures because there's confusion around what a notary is. In a lot of Spanish-speaking countries, a notary is often an important and well-educated person who has a lot of the same abilities and skills as a lawyer. In America, that's not the case, and there are a lot of scam artists trying to take advantage of that. Notaries will try to sell legal services. For that reason, make sure, before you hire someone that they're an actual lawyer and not a notary because it's not the same thing here that it might be in your country.

Even once you've determined the person is an actual lawyer, look at the level of experience and knowledge they have. Immigration is complicated, so it's not for someone who just dabbles in it a little bit at a time. When you have an issue as politicized as immigration, with laws constantly changing, every case will be different in a way that is not true in other areas of the law.

The smallest details can make a huge difference in your case, so you need someone who is detail-oriented and who understands that those details really matter. I've mentioned, for example, that having a criminal record can be a problem, but it's actually a lot more complicated than that. Whether a criminal record is a problem and what type of problem it will be depends not only on the specific crime, but also what you're applying for. Certain types of convictions can automatically disqualify you from certain kinds of immigration status. Even just being charged with certain crimes can be a problem. It could disqualify you, or the official who is adjudicating your application can look at the fact that you've been charged and exercise their discretion in not giving you status. Again, the details can matter tremendously there.

One thing that comes up a lot in removal proceedings is that only certain types of crime make people removable and that a crime has to have the elements set out in the statute. It's not even just a question of whether what you did complies with the statute—it's whether the thing you're convicted of automatically requires the jury to find that you violated the relevant federal statute. In some cases, the state's statute and the federal statute don't match up, so something that looks like it could get you deported might not, for example. A lawyer who doesn't fully understand those little details will not be able to give you the best representation.

Do A Lot Of People Try To Go Through The Process Without Hiring An Attorney First?

Many try to handle their own cases, and I would say that that is a mistake. You might be able to get away with it for some simpler processes, like getting a visitor's visa, but anything more complex, anything that will be scrutinized in more detail, could present challenges. I see a lot of people try to save money by doing it themselves, but it ends up costing them more money because they create problems that they originally wouldn't have had, meaning they're not just paying me to do the form anymore. Now, they're also paying me to apply for a waiver because they committed fraud in the initial application or something along those lines. Or because they introduced evidence that undermines their own case, and now we have to figure out how to overcome that evidence. I definitely, therefore, recommend at least consulting with an attorney, even with a simple matter. A lot of things look simple and then turn out not to be, so it's best to have an understanding of what you'll need to do going into the process.

Common Mistakes Someone Might Make If They Attempt The Process On Their Own

One mistake I've seen people make is not being fully honest with the government. You have an obligation to disclose the answers to the questions that they ask you. An experienced and competent attorney can help you manage how you'll answer questions and present negative information in the best light as possible. Either way, you can't hide information. One thing to keep in mind if you're tempted to do that is that the government knows a lot more about you than you think they do. If you're hiding something, they'll find out about it.

The second mistake is not understanding the limitations on what you might be eligible for or what waivers you might need in order to become eligible. Again, eligibility for anything is complicated. If you have any kind of criminal record, that might disqualify you from what you're looking for, or it might require you to get a waiver. The same goes if you've ever been in the country illegally, if you've ever worked illegally, or if you've ever been deported. If you lack an understanding of what you are and are not eligible for, you can waste a lot of time and money applying for things you aren't eligible for. In some cases, if the government finds that you filed a frivolous application (meaning an application that you were not qualified for) and that it was clear there was no valid legal claim at all, then that can actually penalize you and make you ineligible to file valid claims in the future. Make sure you understand what you are and are not eligible for before you apply for anything.

Clear Benefit To Having An Experienced Immigration Attorney On My Side

You have someone who knows the process, who knows the law, and who will evaluate all of your options so that you can pursue any form of relief you might be eligible for. If you're not eligible for anything, then you can get an accurate opinion about that and figure out how to move on with your life. Knowing the law—knowing how to persuade judges and how to put a case together into what kind of evidence they like to see—will help you present the best possible case.

INDEX

F

G

H

I

NOTES

Made in the USA
Monee, IL
05 November 2026

67387962R00048